# fast thinking: presentation

- ▶ make your case

- ▶ get it across

- ▶ win people over

by Ros Jay

# contents

# introduction

You've got an important presentation to give in a couple of days – maybe even a couple of hours. The clock's ticking, and you haven't even started yet. But it had better be good, because this one matters. You have to sell your big idea, win a major order from a key customer, or maybe persuade your board of directors to invest big-time in a fully integrated website. Or perhaps you have to sell management's case for restructuring to a sceptical staff.

Whatever the objective, you know you should be giving a lot more time than this to preparing the presentation. But life's too fast in the modern business world, and you just don't have that time. So what's the solution? Fast thinking, that's what. And whether the time pressure is high or merely moderate, you need to think smart.

This book is about thinking fast and smart to prepare a presentation in a day or two. You can't possibly do justice to an all-day presentation to 300 people in this time, so that's not what we're about.

This book is about preparing a presentation of between a few minutes and, say, an hour, probably on your own or with just one or two colleagues, to a small audience. This is the most common type of presentation, and it can easily be done in a short time. But if you're working on a bigger presentation and want some last-minute ideas for pepping it up, *Fast Thinking* can help you add gloss.

Sure, it's better to have more time, and this book will tell you what to do with it when you *do* have it. But for now, what you need is the fast thinker's version. You want

 **tips for looking as if you know more than you do**

 **shortcuts for doing as little preparation as possible, and**

 **checklists to run through at the last minute.**

all put together clearly and simply. And short enough to read fast, of course.

Let's assume you have a couple of days to prepare your presentation. Ideally you would have longer, and you would have started early in case some research material took a while to get hold of, or visuals took some time to prepare. But that's fantasy land. You're here, now, with only a day or two left. If you're really up against the clock, you may have only an evening to prepare for a presentation tomorrow morning. If that's the case, you'll find a checklist at the back of the book to help you really step on the gas (see page 78). And for the truly up-against-it, the one-hour version (page 94) will show you how to prepare faster than the speed of life.

So take the phone off the hook, take a deep breath, and don't panic. It's all in here, and this book will get you through the process of preparing for your presentation in as little as an hour, if that's all you've got. Every hour you have beyond that is a bonus – a luxury if you like – so if you have a whole evening to prepare, you've got time to relax ... and even make yourself a coffee before you start.

This book is going to go through the seven key stages of preparing and delivering a presentation.

1  The first thing to do is to identify your objective, so that you can prepare the presentation faster and smarter.

2  After this comes the basic preparation, collecting together all the information you can in the time you have.

3  The next step is structuring the presentation to give it the kind of clarity which makes it look really slick and which drives its message home.

4  After this, we'll look at how you can get everything you want to say into usable note form.

5  Next you need to think about the kind of language you use to be clear in your arguments and to make your audience feel they can relate to you.

6  Visual aids are a valuable part of most presentations, but if they aren't right they can damage rather than improve it. So the next stage is to design your visuals to be really effective.

7  And finally, you arrive at the finished presentation. The last lap involves rehearsal, delivery, handling questions and coping with nerves.

The first thing to do is to identify your objective, so that you can prepare the presentation faster and smarter

# fast thinking
# gambles

**O**f course we all know you should have left longer for this presentation, if only it had been possible. But why? Fast thinking will stop you looking like a fool, and will achieve your objective comfortably. So what's the point of making more time? Well, however good you are at fast thinking, some things take more time than you've got. Basically, when your time is limited, your options are limited.

So what is the downside of preparing for a presentation at full throttle instead of at a steady pace?

> **Research is an important stage of preparing for a presentation. Some research takes time, and therefore can't be done at all when you're up against it. For example, you might want to get hold of a copy of your customer's annual report before you present to them, or talk to various suppliers to get a clear estimate of the cost of a proposal you're presenting to the board.**

- ▶ Your audience is likely to ask you questions at some point. The better prepared you are, the more likely you are to be able to answer them effectively. The corollary is that the less preparation you've done, the greater the chance that they will identify a gap in your knowledge.

- ▶ Visual aids are a traditional ingredient of presentations. While they are often overused (the good news), there are nevertheless times when they lend considerable weight to your argument. Some potentially valuable aids take more time to prepare than you have, and you are therefore missing out on a useful source of persuasive material.

- ▶ Things can go wrong, technically, during presentations. Your notes fall to the floor, shuffling themselves in the process. The slides get out of order. The power supply to your computer fails. Your audience asks you to cover the topics in a different order because one of their number has to leave early. All these calamities are reduced or removed by preparation and practice, and the time to arrange fallback positions to cover likely emergencies.

- ▶ Your own delivery is the key to the effectiveness of your presentation. Unless you are a real natural, you will need time to learn how to deliver your presentation well.

- ▶ For the nervous, the real solution is rehearsal. The better you know what you're doing, the more confident you will feel (stands to reason). So cutting down the rehearsal time will leave you more susceptible to stage fright.

Fast thinking will turn a potentially embarrasing spectacle into a polished, professional and persuasive presentation. But for a truly top-notch, first-class, five-star performance every time in the future, your best chance is to start a good couple of weeks ahead … next time.

**Fast thinking will turn a potentially embarrassing spectacle into a polished, professional and persuasive presentation**

# 1 your objective

One of the first things we tend to do when we're short of time is to stop thinking. We want to get on and *do* something. So we frantically collect up paperwork, start scrawling notes, dig out handout material and trawl through documents looking for something we can turn into a visual aid. It feels more productive – but it isn't. A little calm, clear thinking at the beginning of the whole process will save you a great deal of time later.

And the single most important thing you can think about is your objective. What is the idea you're trying to sell? What is this presentation for? We're not talking general stuff here, such as 'to win an order'. We need to be specific. How about 'to persuade the customer that our website design service is better than the competition'? That's getting better, but it could still be more specific – better in what way? What are this customer's key concerns – cost, effectiveness, technical superiority?

Here's a clear, concise objective, then:

*To persuade the customer that our website design service will attract more visitors and repeat visitors to their website than the competition, and will be easily upgraded as new technology becomes available.*

Now we've set out clearly what precisely it is that we want to achieve as a result of the presentation.

Once you've identified your objective, write it down. This is your touchstone for the rest of the preparation you will do. If any research, information, visual aid or whatever doesn't further this objective, don't waste your time on it.

**BUYING TIME**

Allocate yourself five minutes to think through your objective, and time yourself. If you only have an hour, you could cut this down to three minutes. However, don't allow yourself to take any less time. Tell yourself that, however panicky you are, if you finish early you'll just have to twiddle your thumbs until your five minutes is up. This should help you to give the exercise the time it deserves. Getting this bit right will save you plenty of time later.

# 2 preparation

**P**reparation is a large part of what makes a presentation work. The point of a presentation is to bring the audience round to your point of view, and well-researched and prepared arguments, with data to support them, are a key part of this. So don't be tempted to feel that you are wasting time you can't spare here. You can usefully occupy at least half your available time with preparation, excluding the time you spend physically preparing visuals and writing out notes.

Again, much of this is thinking time, and a cool, unflustered approach is what fast thinking is all about. Just because you aren't doing anything beyond jotting down notes, it doesn't mean you're wasting your time; quite the reverse.

## RESEARCH

Aargh! This sounds like something that takes ages. Well, yes, it can do. But on this occasion you haven't got ages, so obviously it isn't going to take long today. But research is important. This is because if you don't do any research, you can make a real prat of yourself. Let me give you a few salutary examples.

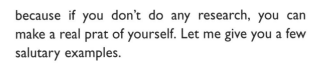

- ▶ **You don't learn the names of the customers you are presenting to, and your boss walks in unexpectedly and asks you to introduce everyone.**

- ▶ **You spend several minutes explaining why it's worth investing in a website only to discover that they already have one – they just want a better one.**

- ▶ **You are asked the cost of a maintenance contract after the installation is completed, and you have no idea.**

Right. So you clearly need to do *some* research. But how little can you get away with? Or, better still, how much can you do in a limited time? Let's begin by identifying the areas you need to research:

1 your audience

2 your product or service

3 shared history

4 facts to support your case.

As you think through each area, jot down any salient points on a sheet of paper.

*Your audience*

This might seem obvious, but there's plenty that can get missed out if you're not thorough. Here are the basics to cover:

- **their names and job titles**
- **their likely attitude to your presentation – are they keen or reluctant to be persuaded?**
- **their level of knowledge – don't throw technical jargon at them if they know little about the subject, or talk down to them if they are experts.**

Luckily, you can answer most of these questions by thinking, or referring to the memo inviting you to give the presentation. You can often make a quick phone call too – an enthusiastic buyer or a boss who has asked you to give the presentation to convince their colleagues will happily fill you in on the background of the other audience members.

If the presentation is to a customer, the more you can learn about their organisation the better. Sales leaflets, background on their current supplier, press articles and so on are all useful here.

*Your product or service*

By this I mean whatever it is you are trying to sell. You might be trying to sell enthusiasm to your staff

### ON-THE-SPOT RESEARCH

If you're good enough at thinking on your feet, you can save a large chunk of the research until you begin the presentation. Start by asking the audience questions, and build their answers into your presentation as you go along. You can't ask things you blatantly should know already ('Sorry, what's the name of this company again?') but a useful tip is to stick to questions about their thoughts, feelings and opinions. Ask them open questions about what they consider the single most important feature of a telecommunications system, or what they most dislike about organisational change.

to get behind a project, or you might want to sell top management the idea of employing three extra staff. But whatever it is, you need to know your stuff. Don't get caught out with simple questions like 'How does it work?' or 'How many people do you already employ in that department?' Customers will expect you to know the basic facts about a product or service you're trying to sell them, such as:

- size
- price

Customers will expect you to know the basic facts about a product or service you're trying to sell them

- colourway
- add-ons/accessories
- performance data
- competition
- delivery methods and times.

and so on.

The good news here is that you should know most of this already. But think it through again. Have new models been added lately? Has the price changed? Or the price of add-ons? If you're selling a project or an impending change to your staff, how long will it take? What exactly will it entail? What will the benefits be?

*Shared history*

Has your audience had any previous experience of the thing you want to sell them? Have they rejected

 thihthih thinkingsfast

### CALL IN THE EXPERTS

A brief, perhaps grovelling, phone call to an expert – inside or outside the company – can save you hours of research at libraries, in books and on the Internet. You could call an in-house technical whizz, a supplier, or perhaps a journalist who specialises in your industry.

it in the past? Have they used it before? Did they ask you to give this presentation or did you offer it? Have they ever seen the product? Has this customer had generic problems with you, such as late deliveries or product failures, which may influence their attitude?

You may well be able to access this kind of information quickly by viewing computer records, or perhaps in the same phone call where you were asking about the audience background. Or you may have notes from meetings, or copies of other people's reports.

*Facts to support your case*

A presentation is all about persuading the audience round to your way of thinking. And your best ammunition for this is hard facts. So you need performance data, costings, timescales, technical information, and so on.

The more facts you have at your fingertips, the harder it is for your audience to disagree with you. And apart from basic product knowledge you don't have to learn the facts by heart. Jot them down neatly on a piece of paper or a notecard, and have them to hand during the presentation.

DECIDING WHAT TO SAY

Don't begin to think about what order you're going to say things in – structure comes later. But this is

## CONDUCT A MINI-SURVEY

Sometimes you need to present evidence showing how people feel or think about something – survey information. For example, nine out of ten shop floor employees would work flexitime if they had the option. If you're pushed for time, you can still conduct mini-surveys of colleagues, friends, customers or suppliers. The best way to do this is by e-mail. Just ask one or two simple, quick questions with a cut-off time for replying.

the time to make a note of all the things you most want to say: the key arguments you'd kick yourself for if you left them out. Suppose your research has identified that your management board has a history of frowning on employing extra staff who don't directly generate more in income than they cost the organisation. In this case you want to be sure to include all your data to back up your assertion that they will each generate double their own salary within the first year.

If your audience is very cost-conscious, you want to focus on the figures. If they are nervous of new technology, you want to include a bit about how easy it is to use, or how the really terrifying thing would be falling behind their competitors technologically. And so on. Jot down all the key points so they are safely on paper instead of floating around tenuously in your head.

Ideally, it helps to write each separate point you want to make on a fresh slip of paper. This takes longer of course (which is why I don't recommend you do it when you're up against the clock), but it does make it easier to keep moving them around when you come to structure the presentation until you're happy with the order.

If you had more time, you would have access to other sources of research information which you haven't got time for now. Here are some ideas for good sources of data when time allows:

- ▶ annual reports
- ▶ press archives
- ▶ management reports and figures
- ▶ trade associations and regulatory bodies
- ▶ government departments, such as the Central Statistical Office
- ▶ surveys – conduct your own or study existing ones
- ▶ interviews.

If you're short of a lot of important data for an imminent presentation, get yourself a copy of one of the companion volumes to this one: *fast thinking: finding facts*.

This is the time to make a note of all the things you most want to say: the key arguments you'd kick yourself for if you left them out

# 3 structure

One of the most convincing ways of appearing practised and professional is to use a clear structure for your presentation. There's nothing worse than a presenter who jumps from point to point, backwards and forwards, interspersing their talk with remarks like 'Oh, yes, I forgot to mention…' and 'Actually, I should have said…', and so on.

When you're pushed for time, a good structure will help you to prepare your presentation more easily and to keep a clear head while you do it. And it will convince your audience that you have really put time into working up this presentation. You obviously take them seriously to have put in so much effort.

There's a simple structure you can use for all presentations, whatever the subject and whoever you are addressing. It divides into four main sections, sandwiched between two top and tail sections:

1 Introduction

2 Position

### INTRODUCTION

Here's your chance to make an impression, grab attention and show how polished and well prepared you are. Your first impression will, of course, be your strongest – so if you make it good, the rest follows far more easily. There's no need to be clever; just be confident and friendly and cover the essentials.

**1** Say hello and thanks for coming.

**2** Introduce yourself.

**3** Say what your objective is (yep, the one you've established already).

**4** Explain how long the presentation will be, and roughly what form it will take. ('I'll spend about ten minutes going through why we need to address the problem of staffing levels in the despatch department, and what the options are. Then I'll outline what I believe is the best option, and why.')

**5** Tell your audience what you want them to do about asking questions (for example, 'Please ask as we go along if you don't follow anything, but would you please save any other questions until the end.').

*Making an entrance*

There is a folklore belief that you should always start a presentation with a witty remark: like so many folklore beliefs it isn't true, but there is truth somewhere at the root of it. The fact is that every speaker needs some sort of acceptance from the audience. If they are to accept what you say, they need some grounds for believing that you are in most ways the same sort of person as them.

A good witty line or a funny anecdote that is not obtrusively dragged in, that is relevant and amusing and gets a big laugh, is an excellent way of giving the audience this sense of all belonging to the same group along with you. However, a funny story or line that fails has exactly the reverse effect and may be very hard to recover from. An opening joke is therefore particularly dangerous with very small audiences, with unfamiliar audiences, when you haven't the time to practise it on colleagues, or if you have any doubts about whether it will get the laugh you intend.

There are many alternatives to humour which will still help you to create an accepting kind of atmosphere. All of these approaches work because they show that you are just as ordinary as the rest of them, and not setting yourself up as a superior person:

- **any expression of personal feelings**
- **some honest self-revelation**
- **a self-deprecating remark.**

Some people believe that you should do something really headline-grabbing at the opening of a presentation. Don't get hung up on this one – you haven't time. If something brilliant springs to mind, great. But it really isn't essential – it's just a bonus.

If you think of something you can do or say that will get a big reaction (such as entering the room through the third-floor window, or appearing in drag) just follow these guidelines.

- **Make the opening directly relevant to the presentation – if it's going to be memorable, make sure that when the audience remember it, they simultaneously remember the point you were making.**
- **Don't make the audience feel nervous or uncomfortable.**
- **Don't use humour unless you are certain it will work, and never crack a joke at the expense of the audience.**

## POSITION

The members of the audience at the start of a presentation are like the horses before the start of a race – scattered all over the place and facing in different directions. The starter at a race meeting has to bring them all up to the line together so that they start level and all go off in the right direction at the same time.

A presenter has to do much the same: if you gallop straight off, you may hurtle along splendidly without realising that you left everybody else behind at the starting gate. So you have to gather your audience together and connect yourself up to them.

The way to do this is to outline the present situation: describe the way overseas distribution is currently organised, or the way the pattern of home demand has been changing, or the way we order stationery at the moment – whatever the purpose of your presentation, it is essential that everyone should start with the same knowledge, and important that you should demonstrate to them all that you know the situation and background. It also enables everyone to focus on the specific part of the present situation which you are addressing. This not only helps comprehension: it also helps you to get accepted by the audience by showing that you understand their situation.

This part of the presentation may take no more than a couple of sentences, or it may need quite a long analysis of how things came to be the way they are. But some statement of the present situation has to be made and agreed upon.

## PROBLEM

This is where you introduce the need for change by showing why the present situation cannot continue, or why it would be unwise to continue it. There must be some significant change or danger or worry or opportunity, or you wouldn't be making the presentation. You need to express this in terms your audience can relate to. Here are some typical catalysts for change:

**thinking fast**

### GET SOMEONE ELSE TO DO THE WORK

If you are a little shaky on the background, and don't have time to research it fully, you could ask one of the audience to state it for you. If it is at all controversial, ask someone with authority: 'Mr Fuller, as Managing Director you've overseen all aspects of this project right from the start. Perhaps it would be helpful for everyone if you could briefly explain the thinking behind it which has brought us to this point? (Then you just nod along sagely as if you knew it all already.) Obviously you shouldn't try this unless you're confident your audience will co-operate.

- Demand is shifting.
- Staff are leaving.
- Competitors are gaining.
- Profits are falling.
- Technology is changing.
- Delays are lengthening.
- Costs are rising.
- Buildings are leaking.

This is the stage at which you dig the hole in which you intend to plant your idea.

A computer salesman once explained, rather convincingly, why his job was very like a missionary's or an evangelical minister's. Both he and they, he said, succeeded by unearthing or implanting some unease, guilt or fear in the person they were trying to convert. He himself did not deal in hellfire and torment, only in business rivals doing things cheaper, better or quicker and some people being left behind, but he felt that the principle was the same: nobody was interested in salvation until they had a fear of damnation.

I am not suggesting anything so extreme; nevertheless if your audience is rather cool it is a great help if you can make them aware, from the

### THE POWER OF PERSUASION

If you have five or ten minutes to spare, read the appendix at the back of this book on techniques for persuading the audience round to your point of view.

very start, of the ways in which what you are about to present is important to them. They arrive prepared to listen: by the end of the first few minutes they should be wanting to know.

This is one of those times when a little thought goes a long way. However pushed for time you are, taking a few minutes to think through what you will say here is always worth it.

### POSSIBILITIES

The two previous sections may be brief: the remaining two form the bulk of the presentation. If you are outlining various options before making a recommendation, you will need to include this section; if you have only one possible course of action to propose you can skip this bit and go straight on to the 'proposal' section below.

Suppose you are asking the board for three new posts to cover what you see as an increased workload. There are other options, too, at least in the board's eyes, and you need to outline these. You could leave things as they are. You could take on just one or two more staff. Or you could even take on four. Your audience needs to understand all these options in order to choose between them.

In this part of the presentation you should aim to conceal from the audience what your preferred option is. Of course they may know perfectly well what it is, but by trying to keep it quiet you will necessarily have to observe the key rules for this part of the proceedings.

**Give facts and not opinions.**

**Be fair to all the arguments.**

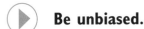

**Be unbiased.**

You need to explain what each option entails, and any statistics or data which back this up. So you need to outline the cost, the timescale, the benefits, and so on. But your audience have to make up their own minds (or at least that's what they should think they are doing), and they can't do that if you keep telling them what to think – they will simply resent you and, by association, your recommendation.

The point about outlining the other options, even if you don't want to propose them, is that your audience will consider them whether or not you do. At least if you include them in your presentation you take the business of analysing them under your control, on an equal footing with your personal recommendation.

In this section you may:

- ▶ **give a product demonstration (or several)**

- ▶ **describe the products, services or packages**

- ▶ **meet objections (before they are voiced)**

thinkingsfast

### FACT FINDING

No matter how pushed for time you are, you are inevitably going to have to come up with certain hard facts for each of the options. You should have collected these during your research stage, but there is always a possibility that you will find you don't have a vital piece of data which you need. To establish the minimum you can get away with, go back to your objective. You need the facts which directly help you achieve this. So, for example, if your objective states that you are demonstrating that your recommendation is the best value for money, you need comparative costs more than you need comparative performance data for all your options.

- compare prices
- give evidence and supporting data
- quote examples.

When expressing the possibilities, you need always to talk in terms of direct benefits to your audience, not merely features of the product or package. To give you a simple example of the difference, a *feature* of a car might be that it has ABS brakes, but the *benefit* is that it brakes more safely, without skidding. Your audience doesn't want to know what each option does, but what it can do *for them*. So three extra staff isn't about getting through the paperwork faster, it's about reducing complaints or improving cash flow.

## PROPOSAL

Now, finally, it's time to come clean about your recommendation. Mind you, it doesn't do to denigrate any of the other options – some members of your audience may have favoured those, and won't want their judgement criticised. So imply that all the options are valid, but show why your favoured one is the best. Obviously if there are no other options this section makes up the bulk of your presentation.

If you omitted the previous section on possibilities, you will now want to do at least some of the following:

- give a product demonstration
- describe the product, service or package
- meet objections (before they are voiced)
- give prices and timescales
- give evidence and supporting data
- quote examples.

## SUMMARY

The ending of a presentation, like the opening, is too important to be left to the mercy of chance or the whim of the moment. True, you may think of an improvement on your planned ending while you are speaking, but it is still vital to have a planned ending to improve on. This does not mean that it has to

thinkingfast

### TOP AND TAIL

If you don't have time to script your whole presentation, at least decide what you will say at the beginning and the end. These are the two most vital moments for making and cementing a good impression.

It doesn't do to denigrate any of the other options – some members of your audience may have favoured those, and won't want their judgement criticised be long, complicated or clever, only that it has to be worked out in advance and rehearsed as well as you have time for.

When working out your ending you must, again, go back to your original objective, since this will dictate it. The ending should normally include:

- a summary of the salient facts and arguments
- a summary of the recommendation
- a proposal for the next step, if the recommendation is accepted, with target dates
- a description or explanation of any handouts you are about to distribute
- thanks for listening patiently.

You will probably want to invite questions at this point as well. Incidentally, you may well want to repeat any key visuals along with the summary, and if you have a single summarising visual (perhaps your only one if you're really pushed for time) you might leave it on display after you have finished as a reminder.

## Questions

You can't stop your audience asking you questions; nor should you want to. It is their opportunity to express doubts so that you can reassure them.

Without that opportunity, any doubt will continue to fester in the minds of your audience. The fear, of course, is that they will ask you a question to which you don't know the answer.

Later on we'll look at how to handle particular types of difficult question. But at this stage, it's a good idea to think through what questions you are likely to be asked. Yes, this is another one of those moments when, even with the clock ticking, you still need to stop doing for a moment and just think. In their position, what would you ask?

Some likely questions you may think of should suggest to you that you go back and put the answer in the presentation proper ('What's the name of your product again?'). But you may well come up with questions which aren't likely, or which are too detailed or specialised to put into the presentation itself, but for which you should nevertheless be prepared. For example, there may be one audience member who wants a detailed breakdown of costs, or specific data on your safety record.

There are two particularly good key ways of spotting likely questions.

▸ **Run through the job titles or remits of the members of your audience – people tend to ask questions related to their own specific field. If the finance director, health and safety officer, or personnel manager is going to be there, this should give you a big clue about what to prepare for.**

> **Phone someone else – a colleague or your boss – who knows something about the subject of your presentation but has a different perspective or a fresh eye, and ask them to give you a quick rundown of anything they think you are likely to be asked.**

The danger, especially if you are preparing your presentation in something of a hurry, is that you will miss the obvious. No one is going to mind if you can't answer detailed, specialised questions on the spot (although it looks great when you can). But it doesn't look so good if you don't know how you arrived at your costings, or how long it will take to deliver the product if the customer decides to place the order. This is what you are investing your time – however precious – to avoid.

thinking smart

### PART OF THE PACKAGE

If you can say everything you feel you need to in about five minutes, but feel you ought to go on longer, why not make the question and answer session seem like part of the allotted presentation time? Introduce it at the beginning as part of your presentation – 'I'm just going to talk for a few minutes first, and then allow your questions to help me make the most of the time we have' – and stay standing up with your last visual still on display; it will look like part of the presentation rather than something else which follows on.

## for next time

If you have time, as I mentioned earlier, it is a good idea to write each point you wish to make on a separate piece of paper. It can also help to write on the reverse of the paper what your source for the information is so that you can find it again easily.

When it comes to structuring your presentation, the first thing to do is to organise all these pieces of paper into just a few groups. You might have one group of points for each of the possible options, for example, or one for cost issues, one for time issues, and one for performance data – along with one for the problem section of the presentation and one for the summary, and so on.

Once you have reached this point, it is very easy to work through the structuring process, moving around whole groups at a time until you feel you have the order right. Individual points can easily be swapped or relocated, and a fresh point added if you think of something else you should have included. But at any given moment your presentation has physical shape which doesn't require you to rely on holding the information in your head where a chance interruption can push it beyond your grasp.

The danger, especially if you are preparing your presentation in something of a hurry, is that you will miss the obvious

# 4 notes and scripts

Now you know what points you want to make, and in what order. You're doing well – you've laid the groundwork for your presentation now. The next step is to find the words to make your point.

When you're in enough of a hurry you may start with a handful of scribbled notes and launch straight into your presentation. From the point of view of the language you will use, that's terrific. But of course it carries the risk that you will miss out certain important – if not crucial – arguments. And that you will get stuck trying to find a good way to express a complex idea off the cuff.

So start with as much of a script as you have time for.

 **In an ideal world (which you don't inhabit just now) you would write out your full presentation and then reduce it to note form.**

- ▷ Failing that, write only notes, but script any important areas you can find time to – the toughest examples, explanations or ideas to express – along with the opening and the close of the presentation.

- ▷ Whatever happens, at least try to script the opening and the close.

Write your notes out by hand on index cards, or using a word processor. You want to include all the key points and any phrases, analogies or metaphors you have identified for explaining complex ideas (see the next chapter). Don't make your notes too detailed, however (as if you had the time), since this makes it harder to find your place in the heat of the moment. You might like to go through and underline the main section headings, or colour-code red for key arguments

## thinking smart

### SCRIPTING SECTIONS

One of the plus points of scripting your presentation in full is that certain points may be difficult to express clearly, and there will be a best way of saying them. A proper script identifies these and finds a clear wording which gets your point across. So identify these sticking points and script at least these sections of your presentation.

**STEADY HAND**

If you type your notes, cut the paper down to a smaller size as this is less obtrusive. If you get shaky during presentations, index cards are better than paper for concealing the fact. Staple your cards or sheets of notes in the top left-hand corner so they can't get out of order.

and green for phrases, for example. Too many colours and underlinings, however, are likely to give you an indecipherable jumble.

Giving a presentation from notes is an excellent way of showing your audience that you have prepared thoroughly, which flatters them apart from anything else. It actually looks more professional and polished than working without notes at all (which can look a bit fly), even if you are one of those lucky people who can do it. You clearly thought your audience were worth the effort. You may know that you were obliged to leave the preparation until the last minute, but they will imagine you have been working on this presentation for several days.

Giving a presentation from notes is an excellent way of showing your audience that you have prepared thoroughly

# 5 language

**O**n the printed page you may get away with all sorts of things you can't possibly say in everyday speech – so don't try and say them in your presentation. It is clarity that impresses people, not long words and convoluted sentences. If you use unnatural spoken language, the people in your audience are likely to feel 'Whoever this person is talking to, it isn't me.' Show you are one of them by speaking their language.

Writing good spoken English can mean writing ungrammatically. In fact, grammatically correct English can be bad spoken English; just count how many times anyone says the word 'whom' to you tomorrow. Very few people can say it and get away with it. Conversely, you can get away with language face to face which you would never allow on the printed page. Slang can be very effective face to face ('Compared with our expenditure on exhibitions, it's peanuts'; 'During peak order times, with our current system, there are frankly far too many cock-ups').

Write this type of language into your first draft – whether it is a full script or you have time only to

### e-STYLE

Written and spoken English always used to differ widely. But in the last few years an overlap has emerged – e-mail English. Almost all of us use a more relaxed writing style in e-mails than we ever do in proposals, letters, reports or even memos. So use this as a guide – write your presentation in the style you would write an e-mail.

make notes – and you can be sure that it will follow right through to the presentation itself.

### USING SPOKEN ENGLISH

OK, this bit is important even if you're racing the clock. In a presentation you are offering a structured series of arguments, and it requires some effort from the audience to follow. The easier you make it for them, the more likely they are to listen attentively and take it all in. So here's a quick rundown of the key techniques for helping them along the way.

▷ **Use short words and short sentences.** Do not say: 'Circumstances occasionally arise involving a situation in which one or more of the contributing personnel wishes to exercise the option of continuing in employment beyond the

Show you are one of them by speaking their language

normal retirement date as specified in their formal contractual agreement, in which eventuality suitable arrangements can be concluded for the further maintenance of contribution and consequent enhancement of eventual benefit.' Just say: 'Sometimes people want to stay on after they're 60. If so they can still stay in the pension scheme.'

- *Avoid abstract words*. Abstract words send people to sleep. They are, by definition, hard to get a concrete grasp on, so they tend to wash over the audience's heads. 'Transportation' is an abstract noun: better to say 'car' if that is what you mean. Don't say 'When you take into consideration...' but 'When you consider...'. Words such as 'situation', 'operation' and 'facilities' should all be banned, and either removed or replaced with more specific, concrete terms.

- *Use active verbs (in other words, 'doing' words)*. It is better to say 'we need your help' than 'your help is needed by us'. Active verbs are more dynamic and interesting to listen to than passive ones. So say: 'The department will meet the budget' rather than 'The budget will be met by the department'.

- *Avoid jargon and technical terms*. Unless you are certain that *every* member of the audience is thoroughly familiar with them, avoid these ruthlessly.

It should be becoming clear why scripting – when you have time – is worthwhile. It is far easier to observe these rules in the methodical atmosphere of a scripting session on the word processor than in the heat of the moment at the presentation itself, working from what notes you had time to fling together.

## AN AUDIENCE WITH NO SCRIPT

Whether or not *you* have a script, your audience doesn't. This makes a big difference to them. When we read, we use the written format – often unconsciously – to help us find our way around the document. We know how much there is left by the thickness of it, we skip the bits we can see we don't want to read, we go back and re-read parts we didn't get first time, we check back a reference we think applies to this section too. But when we listen to a presentation, we can do none of these things. As a presenter, you have to do all this for your audience.

### *Signposting paragraphs*

Keep them posted. Tell your audience what's coming up. Don't just say 'Here's why we should do this…' and then list eight reasons. Say 'There are eight reasons for doing this…'. Give them signposts. Tell them where they have come from, and where they are going. Use plenty of phrases such as:

- 'So that's where we are now. Let's see why we need to change...'

- 'There are three key reasons for this. Firstly...'

- 'There are three options to consider. I'll outline each one briefly, and then we'll look at which is the best...'

- 'I'm going to explain what the machine does first, and then I'll turn it on and let you see for yourselves'.

*Signposting sentences*

Signposting applies to individual sentences as well as to the structure of your presentation. For instance, if you say, 'Dickens, Socrates, Drake, Lincoln, Henry VIII – they all had beards', your audience doesn't know why all the names are being mentioned until the last word of the sentence. When it comes you are asking the audience to go

thinking smart

### PLANT YOUR FACTS

An invaluable device for signposting is the rhetorical question. For example: 'Our present warehouse capacity won't be anything like enough. So what do we do? Well…'. You must have noticed that it is much easier to assimilate information if you wanted to know it than if it's just presented to you. The rhetorical question is a good way of digging a hole to plant a fact in.

back and mentally draw beards on all five of them – if they can remember who they were.

If you say, 'Dickens had a beard, and so did Socrates, Drake, Lincoln and Henry VIII' the audience is drawing the beards on all the time. I'm not saying you can't ask them to make this mental effort, only that you must be aware you are demanding it.

Similarly, if someone tells you 'In the last year Harry Smith has climbed the Matterhorn, swum the Hellespont, crossed the Sahara, run from London to Brighton and shot the Niagara Falls in a canoe, and all this blindfold and with one hand tied behind his back', they may provoke a certain shock effect, but they are asking you to go back and do all those things again in your head in the light of the later information.

### EXAMPLES

Another way to help your audience along is to give them plenty of concrete examples of what you are talking about. Describe how other clients in their position have benefited from changing over to your system, how other companies or divisions have been successful working in the way you propose, or give examples to your board of what you could offer customers if you installed integrated online ordering: 'They could track their orders online, and check the items are in stock. And if they place an order online and then want to speak to us, our call centre can see their order on screen instantly.'

## METAPHORS

Metaphors convert an abstract or difficult idea into a concrete image which the audience can grasp. For example, when we talk about persuading people by 'showing them you are on their side', and then 'leading them over to your side' during the course of the presentation, that is a metaphor which gives you a concrete image.

The one danger with metaphors is mixing them, and making a laughing-stock of yourself in the process. Mixed metaphors combine two or more pieces of visual imagery which don't go together – here are two genuine examples of mixed metaphors, both from journalists.

▸ **'After shooting himself in the foot last week, he has now scored an own goal.'**

▸ **'President Reagan has left a legacy that may yet turn sour in the mouths of those who rode to victory on it.'**

## ANALOGIES

These tend to start 'It's a bit like…' or 'It's as if…'. They are great for explaining complicated or unfamiliar ideas or concepts. Suppose you're trying to explain how white blood cells work. You could say: 'They're a bit like a school of piranha, swimming gently along. As soon as anything alien appears in their river, they descend on it and attack it mercilessly until they've eaten it. Then they go back to drifting in the current again.'

### BUYING TIME WITH EXAMPLES

When preparation time is really short, you may have to cut the length of the presentation itself. I would never advocate cutting it so short that you cannot say everything that needs saying. However, sometimes you can genuinely get your point across in seven or eight minutes – all you have time to prepare – but feel obliged to talk for longer. When you need to fill time fast, examples are a great way of doing it. An audience is always grateful for three or four concrete examples or anecdotes to illustrate key points.

An audience is always grateful for three or four concrete examples or anecdotes to illustrate key points

Despite the slight risk of sounding as if you're reciting by rote, it is still worth scripting your presentation fully if you have time. You don't need to agonise over every word, since you won't actually work from the script anyway. But it gives you a baseline to work from, means that you have found a way of making each point which you can refer back to if no better phrasing comes to mind off the cuff, and means that all the points you want to make are included in the best order.

Many people find that a script gives them a sense that the job is complete, and boosts their confidence accordingly. If you never get beyond note form, there may be a niggling – if unfounded – worry that you have missed something out. The mere act of writing the script is an important mental stage in the process of preparing your presentation.

Once you have your script, *do not attempt to memorise it.* Turn it into notes as soon as possible (we'll look at notes in just a moment). But use the script to refer to regularly throughout your (leisurely) rehearsal time, as a reminder of the points you are making, and an *aide-mémoire* when you can't find a comfortable way of expressing a particular point.

## fast thinking pause

Hang on, we're nearly there.

Despite the slight risk of sounding as if you're reciting by rote, it is still worth scripting your presentation fully if you have time

# 6 visuals

A verbal message which is reinforced with a visual one is stronger than the verbal message alone. This is why visual aids are an important part of most presentations. They help you make your point more strongly and more clearly. At least they should do. Whatever medium you use to present your visuals – PowerPoint, flipchart, OHP or anything else – the guidelines are the same. The extraordinary thing is how few people seem to follow these guidelines in their presentations.

The problem is that while a good visual gives a huge boost to your presentation, a poor visual leaves it worse off than no visual at all. It distracts at best, and baffles at worst. So if you're going to use visuals, make sure you use them well. If you haven't time to do this, don't use them at all.

## DESIGNING VISUALS

The first question when you plan your presentation shouldn't be 'What visuals do I need?' but 'Do I need any visuals at all?' The answer may well be no,

## BUYING TIME

Good visuals can take time to prepare. Simply devising the idea can take a while. So if you're preparing your presentation against the clock, visuals are often the first thing to go. This is great if it stops you cobbling together ill thought-out visuals, but it can mean missing an opportunity to reinforce an important argument. So aim to produce just one visual, and then put all the time you have into making it a really memorable one which reinforces the central message of the presentation.

in which case you have saved yourself a load of time (hey, have another coffee). Here are the reasons for avoiding all visuals.

- ▷ **They take time and thought to design.**

- ▷ **They can divert your attention away from what you want to say and on to how you want to say it.**

- ▷ **They diminish your flexibility during the presentation.**

- ▷ **They can cost money.**

- ▷ **If they go wrong the result can vary from mild confusion to the ultimate in catastrophe and humiliation.**

If you haven't time to use visuals well, don't use them at all

So why do we ever think of using them? Well...

- **A picture is worth a thousand words.**

- **They can portray vividly and instantly things that are impossible to convey verbally.**

- **They can save time (aha! tricky paradox here) – it can be quicker to come up with a visual to illustrate a complex point than to think of a clear analogy.**

- **They create interest.**

- **They lend variety.**

- **They add impact.**

- **They remain in the memory long after the words have left it.**

All in all, the balance generally comes down in favour of visuals (good ones, that is). But it is reassuring to know that there are disadvantages, and many excellent presentations include no visuals at all. If you do have time to include them – however few – think about them at the start and build them into the structure of your presentation. Decide where you need a visual to help reinforce an argument, not just where there's a point which makes you think of a really funny cartoon. A visual which does not back up the argument it accompanies will distract from it.

### THE MISSING VISUAL

One troublespot you need to look out for – even when you're in a hurry – is the visual which isn't there and obviously should be. If you are trying to explain something complicated – from the inner workings of a machine to the comparison of financial statistics – it can beg for a visual to make it clear. In this case, I'm afraid you must provide one.

### THE IMPACT VISUAL

A good discipline for any presentation is to ask yourself what single message you most want the audience to take away with them. This will identify the one visual you most need to include in your presentation. It should be the most visually

thinkingsfast

#### SECOND-HAND VISUALS

So long as a visual is neat and makes its point clearly, that's all that counts. You can scan or copy a graph from a management report, or a diagram from your production development team's files. You don't have to redraw it from scratch. Just make sure you don't breach any copyright by copying from books.

> ## DOUBLE UP
>
> You can save time by using fewer visuals and repeating them. If you reiterate an important point, repeat the visual which accompanied it too.

memorable of all, and is the one you would choose to leave on display at the end of the presentation.

### WORDS ARE NOT VISUALS

How often have you sat through presentations and seen endless visuals listing abstract nouns: PREPARATION, PLANNING, PRODUCTIVITY, PROGRESS and the like? Visuals are not there to provide words; that's your job. You do the words, the visuals do the pictures. Just occasionally they need to incorporate words as labels to help identify what is going on in the picture, but words alone do not constitute visuals. Luckily, you probably don't have time to make this mistake. One way to avoid this trap (for future reference) is always to ask yourself 'What will this visual *show*?' rather than 'What will this visual *say*?'

If you do have to use words – for example to label a pie-chart – write them horizontally. Never use them at any other angle, whatever the temptation.

## KEEP IT SIMPLE

A popular error with visuals is to make them too complicated. It is just about impossible to put too little information on a visual, while including too much is very easy. This is one of the risks with copying existing material – it can need simplifying before it is suitable. If this is the case, and you haven't the time, you are probably better off scrapping the visual than using it as it is. If it is absolutely essential then make the time to get it right.

Some visuals are such a mass of boxes and arrows and feedback control loops that you might as well show a maze from a children's comic ('How can teddy get back to his house without crossing any lines?'). This distracts the audience from whatever you have to say, unless you work through it laboriously. Don't try to include everything in the process on your visual; include only the bits which the audience really wants to know about.

If you have something complex to impart, such as a flow chart, diagram or detailed chart, use build-up visuals which add a section at a time to create a new visual. PowerPoint is obviously the ideal medium for doing this, but you can do it with flipcharts or OHPs too. If you are too rushed to prepare a decent visual in advance, you can draw it on a flipchart as you go along (but make sure you know when you start exactly what you are going to draw).

## DON'T GET CLEVER

When you're deciding what kind of visual to use, opt for the simplest equipment. You haven't time to learn new techniques. If you're not thoroughly *au fait* with PowerPoint, now is probably not the time to learn to use it. Use visuals which will work on a flipchart, and save the PowerPoint until you have more time. A flipchart prepared in advance, using different colour pens, can look very slick.

USING VISUALS

Once you have your visuals (or, for the hard-pressed, your single visual), you must be able to show them in a way which enhances your performance and your message. So here are the principal errors to avoid.

▷ **Unless a visual is blindingly simple, it should at least be referred to, and probably talked through. It is quite astounding how many presenters display and then remove a visual without referring to it or apparently noticing it.**

▷ **Make sure you don't block your audience's view of the visual.**

▷ **Once the visual has made its point it should be removed unless there is a positive reason for keeping it there; otherwise it becomes a distraction.**

## LOOK COOL

If you keep looking to check that the right visual has come up, you will look under-rehearsed and ill-prepared (surely not!). You must be – or at least appear – entirely confident that the next visual will be the correct one.

▷ **Don't use any kind of pointer or cursor if you can possibly help it. If it really is essential as the only means of pointing out something important, move it straight to the spot, keep it still while you are discussing the point, and then remove it completely.**

### PROPS

Of course, you don't have to restrict yourself to two-dimensional images when you're looking for aids to add interest and value to your presentation. Grabbing a handful of objects to pass round as you leave the office can give your presentation that well thought-out and prepared look. It might be the widgets from inside your new machine, or a sheaf of colour swatches, or a sample of the house wine you would offer if you got the catering contract.

The point is, don't forget the 3-D option. Once people can touch and hold something it becomes more real to them. It's much harder to say no to

*Visuals don't have to be two-dimensional*

ordering half a dozen of the really luxurious leather directors' armchairs after you've sat in one rather than merely looked at a photo of it.

## PRODUCT DEMONSTRATIONS

Handing round a swatch is very different from demonstrating a product, but this is something else you may well have to do at a sales presentation. And in the end the product itself will be far more persuasive than all the rest of your presentation put together. But its ability to persuade the buyer to sign the order form relies heavily on you.

Just about the worst thing that can happen during a product demonstration is that the product fails to work. So whether you are demonstrating a blender or a computer, on your premises or on the customer's, make absolutely certain that the product is working and that you know how to use it, and have any accessories or materials you need to demonstrate it fully.

No matter what the time pressure, don't go into a product demonstration without testing it out yourself first. In a sales presentation this is the core of the whole thing, and you should give it top priority. If the demo is bad, you will probably lose the sale. So here are the key guidelines you'll need to follow.

## STANDARD FARE

Remember that standard sales literature such as brochures and price lists make perfectly good presentation handout material with no preparation at all on your part. They are often better than any alternative you could have come up with even given more time.

A handout makes it much harder for your audience to forget your presentation after they've left

- ▶ **Treat the product respectfully – don't slam the doors, or toss a small product nonchalantly from hand to hand.**

- ▶ **Don't talk and demonstrate at the same time. Talk before and after the demo, but shut up while the product is doing its bit.**

- ▶ **Let the customers have a go at using it.**

- ▶ **Encourage questions – you want any doubts brought to the surface so that you can answer them.**

- ▶ **Provide backup literature.**

### HANDOUTS

A handout makes it much harder for your audience to forget your presentation after they've left. They'll think of it when they see the handout – even if they're only thinking about what the hell to do with the damn thing. Providing a handout also gives the impression you've been doing your

> ## BUYING TIME
>
> How about handing out something which you can go out and buy quickly? I've handed out toffee apples before now to reinforce a presentation for which they were relevant.

homework. And on top of all that, of course, it should also contain a message which reinforces what you were saying in the presentation.

- ▸ **What will your audience want you to hand out? They may want price lists, backup information, sheets of performance data and so on which you didn't elaborate in detail during the presentation itself. Make sure you have thought of anything they are likely to want.**

- ▸ **If you're in a hurry, you can hand out previously printed material, or scan, copy or take digital photographs (making sure you don't breach anyone's copyright).**

- ▸ **Choose material which is hard for the audience to throw away. A beautiful photo, a miniature sofa, or a sample of the ingenious new giggle-widget that makes your product's performance so incredibly smooth are all harder to throw away than a piece of paper.**

## HANDOUTS

If time is short, providing just one handout will make a big difference. Print out your key points on a single sheet, in a large enough point size to fill the page without cramping it. Hand this round at the end of the presentation as an *aide-mémoire* for your audience.

## for next time

If you have time, it's worth thinking through your handout material more fully. What do you really want the audience to take away from the presentation? Have you used any high-impact visuals which you could reproduce? Do you have product samples you can give out? Handouts do a valuable job, so give them the thought they deserve.

Find ways to make it harder to throw away or even file away the handout. Laminate a really good cartoon you used as a visual so people can pin it up on the wall. Or find something relevant and memorable, even if it isn't permanent – from food or fresh flowers to a packet of tissues.

**Choose material which is hard for the audience to throw away**

# 7 the presentation

## Delivery

When you're giving a presentation to a relatively small group the whole matter of delivery ought to be simple. You just talk as you would if you were chatting off the cuff, or making a point in a meeting. Curiously, though, most of us find this hard to do. As soon as we are in the more formalised setting of a presentation, we adopt a different tone.

The key to a good delivery, therefore, is not to do anything specific, but simply to avoid this formal, grown-up voice. Alongside this, there are half a dozen particular mannerisms to avoid, which often creep into presentations despite being absent the rest of the time.

- *Mumbling.* It's better to be too loud than too quiet.

- *Gabbling.* Watch the tendency to speak faster than usual if you are nervous, and especially if you are a fast talker anyway.

### AND NOW THE GOOD NEWS...

While I would never advocate preparing a presentation at the last minute if you can avoid it – as I'm sure you wouldn't either – you might find it reassuring at this juncture to know that you have given yourself one advantage. It is easier to sound natural when you speak off the cuff than it is when you spend a long time preparing. Even if you work from notes and not a script – as you always should for a small presentation – repeated rehearsal over time leads to the danger that you will end up almost word perfect in your head. This can lead to a stilted, over-practised delivery.

- ▹ *Hesitating.* Excessive pauses, usually filled with '...er...'. Apart from being tedious to listen to, these almost always suggest that you have not rehearsed sufficiently (heaven forbid).

- ▹ *Catch-phrases.* 'As I say...', 'Basically...', '...like...', '...you know', 'and that sort of thing...'. These phrases are fine in themselves, but if you use them so frequently that they become a verbal mannerism they can distract your audience. (I had a history teacher at school who used to say 'you know what I mean?' so frequently that it became a great game to count the repetitions each lesson and see if she could beat her last record. I can still remember to this day that her all-time record was 23 in a 40-minute lesson, but I remember nothing at all about the corn laws.)

Watch the tendency to speak faster than usual if you are nervous, and especially if you are a fast talker anyway

## REPEATING YOURSELF

A close friend or colleague will be able to tell you instantly if you have any noticeable and distracting verbal mannerisms such as catch-phrases. Just ask someone you know will give you an honest answer.

- *Poor eye contact*. Do your best to look at people as you would in normal conversation. Make natural eye contact with everyone – not just the person in the middle at the front who you feel is on your side. People will naturally follow your gaze, and if you keep looking at the ceiling, so will they.

- *Mannerisms*. Like verbal mannerisms, frequent physical mannerisms such as scratching your ear, or trying to put your hand in a pocket you haven't got on this outfit, will distract the audience. Don't get hung up on removing every personal gesture: just be on the lookout for frequent distracting habits, especially those you only acquire under stress such as foot shuffling or manically adjusting your glasses.

- *Swallowing words*. This is a mannerism which you are unlikely to detect in yourself (assuming you have it) unless you make an audio recording of your presentation. It is generally the last word or two of each sentence that gets swallowed, and it gives the impression that the presentation is repeatedly grinding to a halt. Once you hear yourself do it, however, you should find it an easy habit to overcome.

## REHEARSAL

Rehearsal is essential for several key reasons.

- ▶ It shows up whether there are chunks of your presentation which don't work, are too long, or don't make sense.

- ▶ It gives you a chance to practise your delivery.

- ▶ It means you can time your presentation (but bear in mind that you almost always go faster in the real thing).

- ▶ It helps reduce your nerves – once you know what you're doing your fears subside.

- ▶ It gives you a chance to make sure that any technical equipment such as PowerPoint will work smoothly and slot into the presentation easily.

**thinking smart**

### BUYING REHEARSAL TIME

Go to work by car if you can, even if you don't normally. Unless you are remarkably unselfconscious you won't want to rehearse out loud in the train, but you can practise your presentation aloud in the car all the way to work. Or you can tape the presentation if you have time and then play it back to yourself in the car.

However little time you have, make time to rehearse if you possibly possibly can. Don't just go through the presentation in your head (although this helps as an extra while you're travelling, for example). Hold your notes in your hand, and stand in front of a mirror. Tape record yourself (if you have a dictaphone you can do this really quickly). If you can manage it, rehearse in front of a colleague, friend or partner and ask them to be honest in their comments. But you must rehearse, or all the rest of your preparation could go to waste when you gabble through the presentation, or the visuals come up in the wrong order, or you burst into tears with panic, or your presentation lasts all of 90 seconds.

## QUESTIONS

The vast majority of questions are very simple to respond to. They will be straightforward requests for information, which you will be able to impart. But occasionally someone will ask a question which contains a hidden doubt, or a challenge. So here's a quick rundown of the most common types of difficult question, and how to respond to them.

## for next time

There are, ideally, three stages of rehearsal.

▶ Run through your presentation a couple of times on your own, in front of a mirror and with a tape recorder. Make any changes you feel are necessary as a result of this, and practise improving your delivery or dropping any repetitive mannerisms.

▶ Ask someone else to watch your presentation for you and to make comments. Ask them to be honest but not overly picky. If you find speaking in front of people painful and nerve-wracking, you are aiming for a competent, professional delivery. You don't want a colleague who will keep criticising until you have the public speaking prowess of an experienced politician or actor.

▶ Finally, if you possibly can, rehearse in the physical location where you will be giving the presentation. This final rehearsal can often wait until the morning of the presentation. You are checking that all the equipment works, that the acoustics in the room don't cause your voice to disappear or overpower, that there are no unexpected distractions to prepare yourself for, and so on. Technical problems, in other words.

However little time you have, make time to rehearse if you possibly possibly can

## The concealed objection

It may indeed be only thinly concealed: 'Won't this mean weekend working?', 'Why is the price so high?', but it can be dealt with according to the standard rules for handling objections.

- ▶ **Don't get defensive.**
- ▶ **Make the objection specific – ask what makes them feel the price is too high, for example.**
- ▶ **Put it in perspective – for example, 'It may mean some weekend work, yes, but only Saturdays, and only once every couple of months'.**
- ▶ **Give the compensating benefits – 'and the new system will mean that there's no more coming in at 7 o'clock every morning'.**

## The test question

This is designed to probe your knowledge and experience: 'What are the stress characteristics of this new alloy?' The golden rule is not to try bluffing or excusing your ignorance. If you don't know, say so, and promise to find out for the questioner. Then make a note and keep your promise.

## The display question

Quite often a questioner's real motive is to show their colleagues how well informed they are.

Nothing will make them happier than to have their expertise publicly commended, so don't be afraid to agree and tell them how clever they are. 'Of course you're right. I didn't mention it because it's too technical for some people and, as you'll know, it doesn't affect performance.'

*The challenge question*

You make an assertion which trespasses on the territory of one of the audience. It is best to retreat immediately and with deference, concede them full territorial rights, and perhaps consult their wisdom. 'I'm sorry, of course I was only talking about the US market in general, not the US market for hot water bottles, which obviously you know much more about than I do. What in fact has been the sales trend over the past two years?'

*The defensive question*

Something you are proposing may mean a cut in staff, budget, status, authority, patronage or perks for one or more of the audience. 'What makes you think we can trust area managers to do their own purchasing of technical equipment?' may in fact mean 'Central purchasing is the part of my job I enjoy most, quite apart from all those bottles of Scotch around Christmas, and I'm damned if I'm going to let you take it away from me'. One way to deal with this is to question the questioner ('Could you explain your concern a little more fully?') and get them talking more, and then if you have difficulty dealing with the point at the factual level try to throw it back to the rest of the group by asking them to give their experience – do they feel area managers are up to the job? On what basis are they making their judgement?

With any kind of difficult question, your first reaction should be to quell any emotional response you may feel rising in you, and your second should be to explore the question and ask the questioner to elaborate or refine it. You then have the following options.

- ▶ **Answer the question.**
- ▶ **Admit ignorance and promise to find out the answer (and do so).**
- ▶ **Defer it to deal with privately at greater length afterwards (and make the time for it later).**
- ▶ **Refer it to an expert colleague if you have one with you.**
- ▶ **Throw it back to the person who asked it.**
- ▶ **Throw it back to another member of the audience.**
- ▶ **Put it up for general discussion.**

However bad your nerves are before a presentation there is a cure, although I have to tell you that the more time you have the more effective the cure (sorry about that). The key lies in understanding what causes an attack of nerves. And the root cause is fear. Fear of what could go wrong – from you drying up to the PowerPoint slides playing up. The more remote these failures and catastrophes seem, the more remote will be your fears. This is why you often notice a couple of minutes into a presentation that you're not nearly as nervous as you were just before you began: things are going fine, you realise you're not making a prat of yourself and the visuals seem to be co-operating normally.

If you can minimise the likelihood of things going wrong, you will minimise your fears. Of course there will still be a small irrational panic at the very back of your mind, at least until the presentation is under way, but it need cause no more than a touch of adrenalin which simply keeps you on your toes.

Your best bet is to rehearse as thoroughly as you can. But even when you have plenty of time, you will still want to take other precautions. And when

The better you know what you're doing, the less nervous you will feel you don't have as much rehearsal time as you would like, this becomes even more important. Your motto should be: be prepared. Expect disaster, consider every possible emergency or embarrassment you can, and plan for it. The checklists which follow should be a big help, but you will also want to consider one or two other classic stress-inducers.

- *Notes:* staple these together so they can't get out of order, and have a spare copy as back up if you have time to prepare them.

- *Signs of nerves:* actually no one cares if you look nervous so long as you still do the job well. But we often fear appearing to be nervous. If you are inclined to shake at the start of the presentation, memorise the first few points so that you don't have to look at your notes.

**thinking smart**

### DIFFICULT QUESTIONS

If these are your particular bugbear, get someone to role-play a question and answer session with you and brief them to make their questions as difficult as possible. That way, the real thing will be a breeze by comparison. If time is tight, call up a colleague and get them to interrogate you down the phone.

As far as coping with the physical symptoms of nerves is concerned, try to eat before the presentation. Don't binge, but a light breakfast or lunch will help (unless you really think you'll bring it straight back up). Nerves are always worse on an empty stomach. And on the subject of food and drink, don't mix alcohol and presentations. If you must have a drink, have it now.

You may also find relaxation exercises helpful. The way to reduce stress is to relax, and slow breathing is a quick fix for this. Here's an exercise which you can do moments before your presentation.

1 Sit down if possible, but you can do this standing up if necessary.

2 Relax your arms and hands. If you're sitting down, put your hands in your lap.

3 Close your eyes if you can, but again this isn't essential.

4 Breathe in through your nose, slowly, to a count of five. Breathe in as low down as you can, pushing out your diaphragm and stomach.

5 Breathe out through your mouth to a count of seven. If you are sitting down, don't slump as you breathe out.

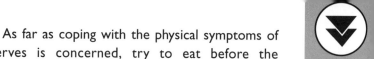

**6** Allow your breathing to return to normal and open your eyes.

You can repeat this at intervals as often as you need to, but always let your breathing return to normal in between. If you don't, you may

thinkingsmart

### BE REALISTIC

Almost all of us suffer from nerves to some degree. But if you are one of those who reacts very strongly, to the point of being sick or passing out, design a presentation where there is as little as possible to go wrong. Given plenty of preparation time, copious rehearsal will help you. But if this isn't possible, cut out anything nerve-wracking that you can. For example:

- Forget the flipchart: devise just one visual with plenty of impact.
- Keep the presentation as short as you can and fill out the time with a question and answer session.
- Bring in a colleague to do part of the presentation for you (the moral support alone is a big help).
- Don't distribute handouts – put them on the table in advance and invite the audience to help themselves later.

Analyse what it is that worries you most, and eliminate or minimise it. You should really notice the difference in your stress levels.

hyperventilate. This doesn't matter at all, except that it can make you feel a little light-headed, which may make you more nervous rather than more relaxed.

## CHECKLISTS

We all know things can go wrong at presentations, and we've all seen it happen to other people. When you prepare in a hurry, one of the biggest worries is that this time it will be your turn to feel like a prat. And of course, the risk really is greater when you have little or no rehearsal. So here are a few checklists to cover the most likely problem areas. Run through these shortly before your presentation (in other words now) to make sure you have everything covered, and again at the very last minute.

There are five main areas to consider:

1 interruptions

2 staging

3 equipment

4 appearance

5 last-minute checks.

Analyse what it is that worries you most, and eliminate or minimise it

### Interruptions

- ▶ **Arrange for phones to be diverted during the presentation.**

- ▶ **Make sure someone is briefed to prevent anyone barging into the room, and put a sign on the door.**

- ▶ **If anyone else regularly uses the room, check they know it will be out of bounds. Include in this not only colleagues but also cleaners, window cleaners, catering staff, postal staff, and so on.**

- ▶ **Check there are no regular interruptions such as fire alarm testing, or break time in the school playground just outside the window. If there are, try to reschedule the presentation.**

- ▶ **You cannot prevent every possible interruption. The golden rule if you are interrupted is to acknowledge the fact. Don't try to talk through the fire alarm test – wait for it to stop.**

### Staging

- ▶ **Make sure you have enough chairs, including a couple extra in case someone else decides to come along too. Arrange the chairs in an arc facing you.**

- ▶ **Check there will be a table for your papers, handouts, briefcase and anything else you have. You may also need another table for equipment, such as a working model or your computer.**

- ▶ **Don't put any barrier, such as a table or desk, between yourself and your audience, unless you are obliged to present around a large boardroom-style table.**

- ▶ Don't stand with your back to a window or you will appear in silhouette to your audience.

- ▶ Sit in each of the chairs in turn to make sure that the view of you or any visuals is not obscured.

- ▶ Make sure you know how to dim or black out the room if you need to.

- ▶ Try to make sure that if there is a clock in the room, you can see it but the audience can't.

- ▶ Except for the most informal presentation, it is better for you to stand. It looks more professional and is a mark of respect to your audience. If you find this very nerve-wracking, and are aware of a tendency to shuffle your feet distractingly, make sure there is a table positioned where you can lean back on the edge of it. (Don't sit on it properly, however, as this will look too casual.)

## Equipment

- ▶ Test all your equipment in advance.

- ▶ Test it all again *in situ* immediately before the presentation.

- ▶ Make sure you know exactly how to operate your equipment and are confident with it.

- ▶ Find out – if you don't already know – what is most likely to go wrong with the OHP, PowerPoint, demonstration model or whatever you are using. And make sure you know what to do when it does.

- ▶ Make sure you have spares of everything you could need – backup disks, spare bulbs, spare batteries, handouts, pens and so on.

## KEEP IT SIMPLE

The less equipment you have, the less can go wrong. If you're in a rush, minimise the equipment. If your presentation calls for a demonstration, you must give one. But do you really need to use PowerPoint? Would a couple of enlarged printouts neatly attached to a flipchart be just as good? And do you really need the OHP, or would a prepared flipchart make the point just as well? Go back to your original objective again and see if the equipment is helping you to meet it, or simply putting obstacles in your way.

*Appearance*

The most important rule is to dress appropriately. All organisations have their own dress codes; a large firm of management accountants will dress very differently from a small company of record producers. People like people who look like them, so adapt your outfit to tone in with your audience's style. Get it ready the evening before the presentation. You want people to remember you for your presentation, not your appearance, so avoid extremes in:

- **fashion**
- **smell (strong perfume or aftershave)**

- ▶ **jewellery and accessories**
- ▶ **large patterns and bright or even lurid colours.**

For your own comfort you should also avoid:

- ▶ **new shoes or clothes that haven't been worn in**
- ▶ **tight clothes which inhibit your movement or gestures.**

You may feel that you want to give yourself an additional air of authority, especially if you've had to prepare in a rush and are less confident underneath than you'd like to be. You can do this by wearing or carrying certain items:

- ▶ **a jacket**
- ▶ **the darkest neutral colours that suit you, such as charcoal or navy**
- ▶ **good-quality clothes and accessories**
- ▶ **a good pen**
- ▶ **smart earrings for women**
- ▶ **heels on women's shoes – not totally flat, but not too high.**

### Last-minute checks

The venue

- ▶ **Check all the equipment is working.**
- ▶ **Make sure it is set up and ready to go.**
- ▶ **Check the position of the screen for maximum visibility.**

- If you are using any kind of lectern or stand, check it is at the right height.

- If you are using any sound effects, check the sound levels.

- Have a list of props, equipment, handouts, your notes etc., and check off everything on the list.

- Get a glass of water if you want one.

- Check you can locate and operate: lights, air conditioning, heating and windows.

- Check the phone is diverted and any likely interruptions have been forestalled.

- If you are on unfamiliar territory, check you know your way to the reception, lavatories, coffee machine and phone – not only for you, but also because one of your audience members may ask you for directions.

Yourself
- women: earrings, make-up, skirt (not hitched up)

- men: tie, shirt (tucked in), flies

- both: hair, nose, teeth.

... AND FINALLY

Have a spare set of notes, for peace of mind, if you can possibly find the time to write them out or copy them. And armed with all the preparation and advice in this book, you should be more than ready to go out there and knock 'em dead.

It's worth carrying a kit with you to fix most things that could go wrong. You may not have time to put much together this time, but here's what to put in your kit in future. Once assembled, you can take this to any presentation with you, so it includes some items which may be more useful for slightly larger presentations. But then again, you never know when you'll need them...

- basic tools – hammer and nails, adjustable spanner, Stanley knife, screwdrivers (flathead and crosshead)
- gaffer tape (to tape down trailing leads that could be tripped over)
- PVC tape
- masking tape (to write on for labelling things)
- fishing line (to tie things invisibly)
- tape measure
- Blu-tack™
- spare felt pens and highlighter pens
- drawing pins, wire, safety pins
- nail scissors
- needle and thread
- spare tie for men/spare tights for women
- comb, mirror
- headache pills.

Have a spare set of notes, for peace of mind

# read this if you have time

### PERSUASION

Even if your customer is internal and not external you're still selling your idea – your way of doing things – to the boss, the board of directors or whoever. And selling is all about persuading people to see things from a particular perspective which will convince them to buy, or adopt the scheme, or agree the purchase or whatever it is you want your presentation to achieve.

There are two key stages in persuading people round to your way of thinking.

1 Show you're on their side.

2 Lead them over to your side.

*The psychology*

The process of listening to a presentation is more emotional (albeit unconsciously) than you might think. The audience needs to feel that you understand their position. In a sense, it shows that you accept them; it puts you both on the same team. This feeling of acceptance is surprisingly important, even to the most hard-bitten business people. In other words, you have to start by convincing them that you're on their side.

Once you're standing alongside your audience – they've accepted you and they're confident that you've accepted them – you can gently start to lead them where you want them to go. You can explain things from their perspective and guide them towards the right decision. They're much more likely to listen to you when you're standing next to them. If you were miles away shouting 'Come over here – it's much nicer, honest!' they could reasonably ask 'How do you know? You don't know what it's like over here.'

So that's the key to the psychology. Don't stand in your entrenched position shouting 'Come here!' If you want them to agree to the idea you're presenting, you have to do the work. Go over to them, take their hand and lead them back to your position.

*Show you're on their side*

▶ **Talk from their point of view.** Always describe their position and their problem, and make it clear that you accept it as such. Never give the impression (even if it's the truth) that you don't see their problem as a problem at all. Suppose the board has asked you to give a presentation. They're not happy with the cost of the food in the canteen; they think it's unnecessary to provide such a wide range at such a generous subsidy. You, on the other hand, think it's the least they can do for their hard-working and loyal staff. You should still explain the problem as they see it. Once you do that, they'll feel you're on their side; so they're far more likely to believe you when you explain later on that, unfortunately, any change in the arrangements would lead to more problems than it would solve.

▶ **Be objective.** Your own credibility is vital. No one is going to allow you to lead them round to your way of thinking if they don't trust your judgement. If the data suggested a different route, you would take it; you're only recommending your own product because you genuinely consider that it matches the criteria more closely than the others: that's the feeling you want your audience to come away with. So avoid subjective words like 'best' – choose an objective alternative. Say it's the 'fastest' or the 'most accurate'; these are statements you can prove. Keep away from fancy adjectives – 'its incredible speed' or 'stunning performance'. It's far more persuasive to specify: 'speeds up to 120 mph' or 'performance which, in tests, was consistently 6 per cent above its nearest rival'.

### Lead them over to your side

So, by the end of the *position* and *problem* sections, you're standing shoulder to shoulder with your audience. They know you understand their situation and their needs. You have shown them that your judgement is sound and your information accurate. Now it's time to examine the possibilities. This is where you start to lead them back over to your side. But do it as if you were treading on eggshells.

- *Be fair.* Treat all the options fairly. If one of the other *possibilities* works out cheaper than the one you're recommending, don't attempt to hide the fact. It's not worth the risk of getting found out – which you almost certainly will. A false statement or the suppression of a relevant fact is like the thirteenth chime of a clock: it isn't just obviously wrong in itself; it also casts doubt on the previous twelve. If, on the other hand, the audience sees you being scrupulously fair, they will have far more faith in your judgement, and be happy to follow you to whatever conclusion you decide to lead them to.

- *Don't dismiss the other possibilities*. Your audience considers all the possibilities to be viable options. That's why you're listing them. If someone wants to soft-boil an egg for their breakfast and is deciding how long to cook it for, you might suggest three minutes, four minutes, four and a half, or five. But you're not going to bother suggesting they get up at 5 o'clock in the morning, coat it in wax so it can't breathe and leave it in the sun for three hours while they go back to bed. You know that option isn't in the running. Never forget that your audience is giving serious consideration to all the other possibilities. So if you criticise any of the options, however subtly, you are in effect insulting their judgement.

- *Give the audience an excuse to change their minds.* Suppose you're giving a presentation to the whole board, half a dozen or more people. Some of them may already have expressed strong views on the subject which your presentation is about. You know what people are like (we're back to the psychology again) – they don't like backing down. So give them an excuse. Explain that they are absolutely right that, for example, this new project will mean a lot of overtime, but that it will also make their jobs more secure. Now they can say 'You see: I was right. Hard work. But, of course, if there are long-term benefits we didn't know about...'.

- *Put your preferred option last.* Your approach to the possibilities you've laid out may vary. For a sales presentation it may well be that the only option you'll be happy with is the one you're recommending. If you're giving an internal presentation you might have a first choice, but several other options you consider to be perfectly acceptable. So don't back yourself into a corner by making one clear recommendation if there are others which you would settle for. But whether you're pointing up your number one choice subtly or obviously, put it last. That way it's freshest in your audience's minds at the end of the presentation.

If you express all the relevant points objectively, fairly and honestly, show respect for all the options, and give your audience an excuse to change their minds, then you have maximised your chances of bringing them over to your side. If that hasn't persuaded them, nothing will.

# presentations in an evening

An evening? A whole evening? You're doing fine. You should meet the poor presenter who's busy reading the next section: presentations in an hour. An evening is long enough to cover the essentials, so there's no panic.

The first thing to do is to read this whole book through once. It won't take too long, and everything you need is here. Next, if you need to make any phone calls – for research, or role playing practice with a colleague – do it before everyone goes to bed. I know this sounds obvious, but it's surprising how fast the time can go.

Apart from that, the real question you need answered is 'What should I leave out?' Well, here are a few pointers for trimming down the preparation time to fit your schedule.

 Do as much research as you can on the phone – in other words, pick other people's brains shamelessly. It's much quicker than looking things up. (But avoid any garrulous colleagues who are always impossible to get off the phone.)

- ▶ Keep the presentation as short as it needs to be to put across your argument clearly and persuasively. If this is shorter than you feel it should last, fill the time by coming up with relevant examples and anecdotes. These are interesting, useful, and easy to slot in without any restructuring of the presentation. You can also make the question and answer session part of the presentation time.

- ▶ Script the opening, closing and any complicated arguments or ideas only – just start with notes for everything else.

- ▶ Save time on visuals. Some things really need a visual to illustrate them, and of course you may have to give a product demonstration. But exclude any visuals which aren't vital. If you have time later, you can always add visuals back in. But generally, aim to have just one really good visual with real impact.

- ▶ Don't trim down rehearsal time more than necessary, and if you have a whole evening aim for an absolute minimum of two full run-throughs (more if you're using visuals or props). Make changes after the first rehearsal and incorporate them into the second run-through.

You should find that this leaves you comfortable time to put together a professional and persuasive presentation, while still leaving you hoping for more preparation time for the next one. The important thing is to relax and not panic. An evening may not be ideal, but it is a perfectly realistic timespan.

# presentations in an hour

You're not sure how you found yourself here, but now you're in this pit you need to start clawing your way out fast. Even though it may well be sheer pressure of work which has prevented you starting on this presentation earlier, the odds are that this got moved to the bottom of the pile because you know you're pretty good at thinking on your feet. Excellent. You'll need to be.

If you only have an hour or so, what can you usefully do to look good and polished, and to win your audience round to your view? Here are the vital stages – read them all through once before you begin. Oh, all right, I know you won't really do that. But at least read point 7 before you start.

1 Spend the first three minutes thinking about your objective (see page 14). Yes, yes, I know you haven't got three minutes to waste. It's OK, it won't be wasted.

If you only have an hour or so, what can you usefully do to look good and polished, and to win your audience round to your view?

**2** I suggest you now cut straight to the structure of the presentation, and skip the preparation. Do the research (page 16) as you need it going along.

**3** Jot down the key points you want to make, check them against your objective, and sort them into the right order as outlined in Chapter 3. Mmm, yes, I'm afraid you're going to have to find time to read Chapter 3.

**4** Obviously you're not going to script this presentation, but look through your notes and see which key points need examples, or would benefit from metaphors or analogies to help illustrate them. A few of these will give your presentation both clarity and colour, and are worth the time investment (see pages 50–1).

**5** Read the bit about signposting (pages 47–49) – it makes a huge difference to how professionally your performance comes across.

**6** Forget the visual aids – and anything involving equipment. But if you want to look more prepared than you are you can always do a handout. Just print out your three or four key points in big letters on a single sheet and hand it round after the presentation.

**7** Leave enough time to rehearse the whole thing once right through. This will show up any major problems, identify ideas or concepts you find hard to phrase well, and give you a timing.

**8** Read the checklists (pages 79–84), or at least the last-minute checks (pages 83–84).

**9** If you have any time left, read the bit about handling difficult questions (pages 62–6: you'll probably be leaving plenty of scope for questions).

**10** Relax … and good luck!